W9-AXU-426

First Facts™

Community Helpers at Work

A Day in the Life of a
Child Care Worker

by Heather Adamson

Consultant:
Sherry Workman, Executive Director
National Association of Child Care Professionals
Austin, Texas

Capstone
press

Mankato, Minnesota

First Facts is published by Capstone Press
151 Good Counsel Drive, P.O. Box 669, Mankato, Minnesota 56002
http://www.capstonepress.com

Library of Congress Cataloging-in-Publication Data
Adamson, Heather, 1974–
    A day in the life of a child care worker / by Heather Adamson.
        p. cm.—(First facts. Community helpers at work)
    Includes bibliographical references and index.
    Contents: How do child care workers start their days?—Where do child care workers
work?—Do child care workers cook?—Do child care workers get to rest?—How old are children
in child care?—Do child care workers ever plan special activities?—Do child care workers use
math?—What happens at the end of a child care worker's day?
        ISBN 0-7368-2504-5 (hardcover)
        1. Child care workers—Juvenile literature. 2. Child care—Juvenile literature. [1. Child
care workers. 2. Child care. 3. Occupations.] I. Title. II. Series.
HQ778.5A34 2004
362.71'2—dc21   2003011447

Credits
Jennifer Bergstrom, series designer; Enoch Peterson, book designer; Gary Sundermeyer,
    photographer; Eric Kudalis, product planning editor

Photo Credits
All photos by Capstone Press/Gary Sundermeyer except p. 20, Image Source/elektraVision

Artistic Effects
Photodisc/C Squared Studios

Capstone Press thanks Kelly Lageson and the children of Shine Daycare, Mankato, Minnesota, for
their assistance in the photographing of this book.

1 2 3 4 5 6 09 08 07 06 05 04

Table of Contents

How do child care workers start their days?

Child care workers wake up early. They get ready before the children arrive. Kelly's first child arrives at 7:00 in the morning. The child's father drops her off on his way to work. Kelly **greets** each child at the door. She helps children find something fun to do.

Fun Fact

About 1.2 million people were child care workers in the United States in 2000.

7:00 in the morning

5

Where do child care workers work?

9:30 in the
morning

Some child care workers work at
child care centers. Others, like Kelly,
work in their homes. Kelly's home
has safe places to play and learn. Kelly
reads to the children. They make **crafts**
using glue and colored paper.

7

11:30 in the morning

Do child care workers cook?

Child care workers make **healthy** meals and snacks for children. Kelly serves pasta and bread for lunch. Everyone drinks milk.

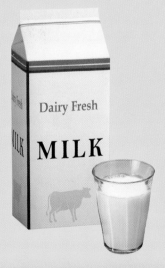

Dairy Fresh

MILK

Do child care workers get to rest?

After lunch, many of the children take a nap. Cribs and cots make nap time **comfortable**. Child care workers do not sleep during nap time. They make sure all the children are okay.

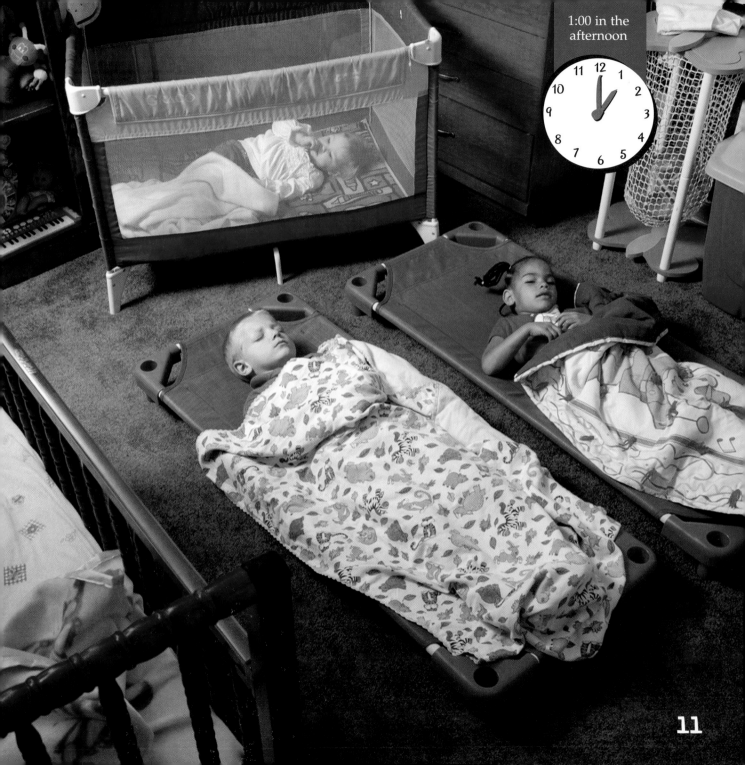

1:00 in the
afternoon

11

How old are children in child care?

Child care workers take care of children of all ages. Kelly watches babies and young children for most of the day. Older children arrive after they finish school. The bus drops them off at Kelly's house.

13

Do child care workers plan special activities?

Sometimes child care workers take children to special **activities**. Today, Kelly and a parent take the children to the park. They are having a birthday party. Everyone walks in a line to the park. The older children carry balloons.

Fun Fact:
Canada celebrates National Child Care Worker Appreciation Day each October.

Do child care workers use math?

5:00 in the
evening

Child care workers use math to plan
costs and buy **supplies**. Kelly records
how many hours she cares for each
child. At the end of the week, she writes
out **bills** for parents. The parents pay the
bills when they pick up their children.

What happens at the end of a child care worker's day?

Child care workers still have work to do after the last child goes home. They plan for the next day. Kelly makes sure there is enough juice for snack time. She puts the toys away. She thinks of all the fun she will have with the children tomorrow.

19

Amazing But True!

Child care workers change hundreds of diapers each week. Some babies use as many as 12 diapers a day.

TV and Stereo
Plays music and videos for kids

Playpen

Infant seat

High chair

Snack

Toys

Craft supplies

Chairs

Table

Books

21

Glossary

activity (ak-TIV-uh-tee)—something to do for fun or learning

bill (BILL)—a written record telling how much money needs to be paid

comfortable (KUHM-fur-tuh-buhl)—relaxing

craft (KRAFT)—something made with your hands; child care workers often help children make crafts with glue and paper.

greet (GREET)—to say something friendly and welcoming when you meet someone

healthy (HEL-thee)—good for you; healthy foods help keep you well.

supply (suh-PLY)—an item needed to do a job or task

Read More

Ballard, Robin. *My Day, Your Day*. New York: Greenwillow Books, 2001.

Gibson, Karen Bush. *Child Care Workers*. Community Helpers. Mankato, Minn.: Bridgestone Books, 2001.

Internet Sites

FactHound offers a safe, fun way to find Internet sites related to this book. All of the sites on FactHound have been researched by our staff.

Here's how:
1. Visit *www.facthound.com*
2. Type in this special code **0736825045** for age-appropriate sites.
   Or enter a search word related to this book for a more general search.
3. Click on the Fetch It button.

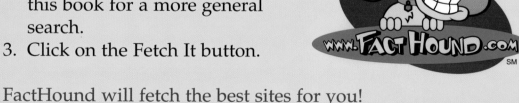

FactHound will fetch the best sites for you!

Index